To Brian.

Hope it was worth the
wait!

Have a great holiday
time & thanks for
your patience

Cheers

Tim

Don't Ask Stupid Questions

There Are No Stupid Questions

ISBN: 978-0-9743620-5-2

For Information address:

Aspen Light Publishing
13506 Summerport Village Parkway #155
Windermere
Florida, 34786

The author can be reached at tim@adaringadventure.com

www.adaringadventure.com

Web design by On Target Web Solutions
(www.ontargetwebsolutions.com)

Printed in the U.S.A.

Acknowledgements

To Skip for being my strength on the occasions when I doubted myself and for offering unquestioned and unwavering support. Without you this would never have happened.

To our families back in the UK for never questioning our decision to leave and encouraging us all the way.

Special thanks go to; John P Strelecky a fine author and even finer person, Michael Watson a great source of motivation, Tom Jelneck at On Target Web Solutions for his brilliant search engine optimization and sound advice and Robert Lussenden for his help and patience with the cover design and layout.

Also, thanks to Hilary for attempting to help me with editing and pointing out that punctuation isn't just random blobs of ink.

Finally to our friends back in the UK that we miss so much and those here in our new country that have made us so welcome.

Thanks.

For Bill & Steph

and Terry & Kate

Table of Contents

INTRODUCTION
July 2007

I think it was about 1995 that I read my first self-development book. It was the classic 'How To Win Friends And Influence People' by Dale Carnegie and after I finished it I vowed to do as the title suggested from then until the day I died. That lasted about a week maybe two and I don't think I won any friends or influenced any other people with my newfound wisdom.

Fast forward to about the year 2000 and after a referral from a friend I picked up a copy of 'Awaken The Giant Within' by Anthony Robbins. Once more I dived in with gusto and thoroughly enjoyed the book. I was determined and committed to awakening my own giant within although at the time I didn't realize he had taken an industrial strength dose sleeping tablet, washed down with a nice Sauvignon Blanc and wasn't getting up any time soon.

Both of these books gathered dust for a year or two more until I once again decided that if I was to live until my 50th birthday and actually start getting the most out of my life I needed to make substantial changes sooner rather than later.

I knew I had to reduce my stress levels, cut down on my workload and try and introduce something that had been lacking from my life for a number of years: Work/life balance.

Initially I opted for books on audio. I wanted to utilize all the downtime stuck in traffic by learning and developing my understanding of what made me tick. The thing that often frustrated me was that a lot of these programs came with exercises included. Usually I would skip past that stage and vow to return when I wasn't driving. I never did. By the time I got to the end I was just too eager to move on to the next earth-shattering, eye-opening nugget that was going to flip the switch inside my head from auto-pilot to manual to actually stop and do anything concrete about it.

It never ceases to astonish me that so many people want to make improvements in their life but so few are prepared to actually do anything to facilitate that change. It is a little bit like joining a gym and expecting the pounds to drop off as you sit at home eating pizza and drinking cold beer whilst lovingly admiring your shiny new membership card.

I'd like you to suspend judgment and remain open-minded as you read this book. Not just about the messages that are in it although of course that would be a good idea too, but much more importantly, about you and your own capabilities.

I have faith in you and an unshakeable confidence that you can be the person that you aspire to be. That you can make the improvements in your life that you want to see and you can make them whenever you want to. That is the good news. The bad news is that there may well be a little discomfort; some doubts and maybe even some rare occasions where you wished you hadn't bothered. The reason for this is that to make lasting change you have to step outside your comfort zone from time to time. Our comfort zone is called that for a good reason. It doesn't require we do anything out of the ordinary, it is familiar and it just feels like it is the right place to be. The down side though is that it can restrict our mental, spiritual and emotional growth and hide our potential from us. It really doesn't have our best interests at heart; it just seems that way.

If you pick this book up and think simply be reading the words you can become a better person you are probably wrong. You need to read them, absorb them and believe in them, not because I or anybody else may say so but because they make sense to you.

You can flick through the chapters in pretty much any order because although some have been positioned for a reason, it really isn't that important. In fact I would be delighted to think that this missive will find its way into the odd bathroom or two. However, I would encourage you from time to time to dip back into the parts of the book that have made the most significant impact on you and re-read them.

About The Questions
The questions that are at the end of each chapter are an integral part of the book. They are designed to make you stop and think.

Read through each question carefully and really give it some thought as to how it applies to you and your life. Do this before you move on to the next chapter. Then decide what action you can and more importantly, will take. Without action nothing will change and if nothing changes then guess what? Nothing changes.

About NLP

NLP stands for Neurolinguistic Programming and I make several references to it in the book. It really isn't that important that you know anything about it, unless of course you want to. It is an umbrella term for all sorts of techniques and methods for helping people change not least of which is something called advanced language patterns. If you want to learn more about NLP then please visit my website at www.adaringadventure.com and click on the Links tab or Google it and wade through (at the time of writing) the 16,000,000+ results.

About The Writing Style

I have been told that I have a strange writing style which lacks correct punctuation and use of grammar. I think the reason for this is that I tend to write as I talk i.e. quickly and without coming up for air too often. My belief is that as you get into the book you will start to get to grips with it and, by the end, be convinced that I am a literary genius the likes of which the planet has never known before. Was that a run on sentence? I have no idea, which is probably part of my problem.

I have thoroughly enjoyed writing this and know that I have learned a great deal about myself in the process. My only wish now, is that it helps you to be the person you want to be and live the life you want to live.

Cheers

Tim

1
The Two Most Powerful
Questions In The World

Children ask better questions than adults. May I have a cookie?
Why is the sky blue? and What does a cow say? are far more
likely to elicit a cheerful response than Where's your manuscript?
Why haven't you called? and Who's your lawyer?

- Fran Lebowitz

The more life coaching I do the more I come to believe that the
quality of our life and those around us is heavily influenced by
the quality of our questions, and by that I do not necessarily
mean the questions we ask of others but the ones that we ask
of ourselves.

I want to tell you about the two questions that I think are the
most powerful in the world. I'm absolutely serious about this, if
you can bring these questions to mind in moments of crisis I
guarantee that you will immediately be better able to deal with
the issue at hand.

The first question is to be used when something has not gone as
planned. It may be you missed a job opportunity or even lost your
own job, it may be something less stressful like losing a round of

game of tennis or not hitting your target weight by the date you set. It can be used in a multitude of different circumstances, and as you play about with it, I'm sure you will choose those that are most advantageous to you.

What Can I Learn From This Situation?
Simple really like most great things, but it does work. If when things do not go to plan you still extract positives and use it as a learning experience then each subsequent event will improve. The problem many people have is a tendency to dwell on the negative rather than on the positive. Most situations do contain a positive even if it's very well hidden. When you become a master at extracting it then you will also be a master at improving yourself and dealing with problems in your stride. Haven't we have all had events that seemed catastrophic at the time that turned out to be blessings in disguise? The firing that lead to starting a business, the break up that lead to a more fulfilling relationship or maybe even that illness that lead to taking better care of your health.

What Else Can This Mean?
This is a question I use on a daily basis because I think it is so valuable. Think of this scenario: You have arranged to meet your partner or good friend for dinner and you arrive on time at the restaurant. The other person still hasn't shown up after 10 minutes and you start to say to yourself "typical, she is always late, she simply has no respect for other people". Not really very useful is it and not very likely to pave the way for a great night?

How about if you asked yourself what else can this mean? Now you have choices. The internal voice could now be saying "she must really care about me because she is obviously taking the time to look her best" or "It really wasn't very thoughtful of me to pick a restaurant that is so dogged by bad traffic I'd better make a real effort to make up with a great night" Both of these are guaranteed to prevent any arguments and make sure you keep things in perspective.

Think and reflect for a moment on the last time that you had an argument with a loved one. Try and briefly regain those feelings by seeing what you saw, hearing what you heard and feeling what you felt. Now recreate the internal dialogue that was going on inside your head.

What are you saying to yourself? Are you asking questions that are helpful or are you asking questions that are likely to exacerbate the situation and lead to an argument? At times like this we often disappear inside and look for evidence to support our opinion that we are perfectly justified in feeling like we do. Well, we have another alternative, and that is to ask, "What else can this mean?" and to put a hugely positive spin on the situation by changing our state and our outlook

Question: What kind of questions do you ask yourself? Are they serving you well?

3

2
Who Is The Most Important Person In The World To You?

"Love yourself first and everything else falls into line. You really have to love yourself to get anything done in this world."

- Lucille Ball

This is a question that I ask most of my coaching clients at some point or another. As you would no doubt expect the answer varies but it usually leads to some deep thought. The thought processes that it invokes are the real reason I ask the question. From experience I know that the answer I am looking for is not the one I am going to get.

I hope that you are taking the time now to think how you would answer that question if your spouse, your child or a friend were to ask you. Think about it seriously. Don't just blurt out the most obvious answer or the answer that you think they would want to hear.

Hopefully after careful consideration you've come to the conclusion that YOU are the most important person to you. It's not your wife or husband or parents or even your kids, it is YOU. Without you everything else literally ceases to exist.

Too many people spend their lives putting other people first and never themselves. This is simply the wrong way round. Of course we want to look after our loved ones as best we can, but without love for ourselves it is almost impossible to offer it to anybody else.

I am sure you are familiar with the aircraft safety process that calls for putting on your own oxygen mask in an emergency before trying to help others. That is because you can't help anybody else properly if you can't breathe yourself. Soon you'd become useless; in fact worse than that, you would become a burden on those around you. Life is like that, by giving away all your resources you soon cease to be a help to those that matter to you or depend on you and you become a liability.

I know a lot of people will think of this as the nonsensical ramblings of a bitter man and will not accept what I am saying. I can understand that but let me tell you a secret. The most efficiently benevolent people on earth still put themselves first. They know that if they don't look after their own mental, physical, emotional and spiritual health then they can't function efficiently.

I'm not suggesting you become self-centered and arrogant or that you neglect your family and loved ones. In fact I am suggesting the complete opposite because when you to decide to be kind to yourself first then you will have more to offer others.

Question: If you accept that you are the most important person in the world, what can you do differently to demonstrate that belief?

3
Comparison Doesn't Deliver Contentment

"When you are content to be simply yourself and don't compare or compete, everybody will respect you."

- Lao Tzu

One of the things that I see with clients that can be frustrating is the insistence that they compare themselves to others when setting goals. They may work in sales and decide that they want to earn more than a top performing peer, or think that to be happy they have to be as slim as a friend or even worse, a movie star, or believe that the only true measure of business success is to generate more revenue than a competitor.

Let me tell you that this practice is doomed to failure 99 times out of 100.

With over 6 billion people wandering around this planet there are always going to be people that are better than you and there are always going to be people that are worse than you no matter how you stack it. By comparing yourself to others, and that goes for either individuals or groups of people, you are handing over control to outside forces over whom you have no influence. What happens if that sales person takes it up another notch, or that friend drops another 7lbs or that competitor suddenly expands by acquisition? I will tell you what happens. You will almost certainly become frustrated or dispirited or perhaps both.

There are a handful of people that can say, unequivocally that they are the best at what they do. Even then, that select band will have their supremacy confined to one tiny area of expertise. Tiger Woods may well be the best golfer in the world but there are a great many people that can run faster, jump higher, think quicker, paint better, write more eloquently, drive faster and whatever other criteria you care to mention and measure.

Do you really think that Tiger sits at home worried because somebody earns more money than him or is stronger, or can do the Sudoku quicker? I doubt it. If he did it would certainly not allow him to focus with such clarity out on the golf course and would lead to a rapid decline in his performance.

There is only one person that you should ever compare yourself to on a regular basis and that is you.

If there are areas of your life that you wish to improve on, then good for you go ahead and set yourself some goals. Then measure where you are now and try and beat that. You have complete control over that and if you continue to improve and move toward your goal then each step on the way will result in a feeling of achievement without a glance over the shoulder to see what somebody else is doing and whether it's ok to feel good or not.

Oh and by the way, it's always ok to feel good about yourself and don't listen to anybody that tells you otherwise.

Question: What unreasonable comparisons are stopping you from being the best person that you can be?

4
Are You Open-Minded?

"I don't believe it. Prove it to me and I still won't believe it."

- Douglas Adams

My clients seem to fall into two very distinct types. There are those that are really into the more esoteric side of what I do such as manifesting, visualizing, meditating etc and those that have no interest in it whatsoever and think it's mumbo jumbo concocted by people that knit their own yogurt and stroke whales for a living.

I can understand and I'm cool with both points of view. We've been brought up in the West to look at things a little bit more pragmatically and analytically than is the case in some other cultures, especially those from the Far East.

We have tendency to see science in absolutes. When we encounter events that don't fit neatly inside a box or we're unable to label them in a way that feels comfortable to us, we dismiss them by either refusing to accept that they could be true or see them as some weird coincidence or one-off freaks of nature. Modern quantum physicists tends not to believe in random acts of nature and neither did Einstein suggesting, "God does not play dice with the universe"

13

Some of the practices such as meditation, yoga, tai chi etc have been going on for centuries in the Far East and there is enough anecdotal and scientific evidence demonstrating that they can be highly beneficial to shake several sticks at.

I'm guessing you feel you are an open-minded person. Most people do you know. In fact I'm amazed disputes ever arise or arguments ever get out of control when the world is so full of tolerant, reasonable and easy going people.

If you doubt that you can manifest the life of your dreams, or if you refuse to accept that visualization aids success or that meditation can help you live longer, why not suspend disbelief and cynicism for 60 days and try one or more out?

If you are genuinely open-minded what have you got to lose? If you see no beneficial changes in your life then you can go back to how you were before, you don't need to buy the loincloth and Buddha statues just yet!

A great many people complain about their life and their circumstances yet few do anything significant to change it. Now you know you have a choice.

Question: How could you practice being more open-minded?

5
The Storm Before The Calm

"A dream is your creative vision for your life in the future. You must break out of your current comfort zone and become comfortable with the unfamiliar and the unknown."

- Denis Waitley

How do you feel when you install a new program on your PC and you don't know how it works? What about starting a new job that you don't fully understand or taking up a pastime for the first time like golf or fishing?

Most people realize that when they step out of their established comfort zone and attempt to do something completely new that, no matter how skilled they are, there is typically a period that feels really uncomfortable and awkward.

However, what everybody doesn't know and I'm here to tell you kind reader, is that this is a good thing.

I often have clients tell me after 2 or 3 sessions that they actually feel more confused and unsure about what they are doing than before they took a coach on. Initially this concerned me, after all my job is to help people get from where they are now to where they really want to be in their life, not to drag them down some dark cul-de-sac, mug them of their cash and dreams and then leave them to find their own way back to safety in the darkness.

However, after this happened a few times I started to notice a pattern that this doubt was frequently followed by significant breakthroughs. It has now got to the stage where I sometimes look for signs of confusion to let me know that I'm about to make a step forward because I now know that out of confusion arises clarity.

The potential tragedy to the uninitiated though is that an increase in uncertainty often makes people draw back from their goals just as they are within their grasp. We have a natural inclination to seek safety and although we are seldom in actual physical danger during the process we can certainly be in mental turmoil and this can feel just as bad to many people.

If we set off knowing that we may well need to pass through this tunnel of confusion to get to our destination then we can meet it with enthusiasm because it tells us that we are on the right path.

The anomaly though is that the sheer act of accepting discomfort rather than fighting it will actually reduce it. Also, each time you do this you actually start to stretch your comfort zone and when you realize that you have the power to do that, the world truly is your oyster.

Question: What could you ultimately achieve if you just keep on going the next time you feel awkward or confused?

6
There Is No Criticism Only Feedback

"To avoid criticism do nothing, say nothing, be nothing."

- Elbert Hubbard

There is a pre-supposition in NLP (Neurolinguistic Programming) that I like to use in coaching that says there is no failure only feedback. I'd like to add to that by saying there is no criticism only feedback. Imagine if every time somebody criticized you, you smiled, thanked them for the feedback and moved on?

A few years ago I was working for a rather large blue chip organization in the UK. It was my first spell with the company and I was keen to get into management, as I believed I had the requisite tools to do a good job. I applied for management development confident that it was a formality but got turned down. I was crushed, I mean really knocked back by this, I couldn't see any reason why they wouldn't want me leading a sales team and barely heard the reasons why when they were delivered to me. I was told I was too negative and needed to tow the company line a bit more instead of shooting off on my own tangents etc. It was recognized I was a team player and good salesperson but also known that if things weren't going too well

I would moan and whine to the rest of the team and not make it easy for those above me.

Of course I knew that this was all nonsense and for a few months carried on as before. Then one day I was reading the Jack Canfield book 'The Success Principles' and was struck by an old proverb that he made mention of:

If somebody tells you you're a horse, they are insane.

If 3 people tell you you're a horse, there is a conspiracy.

If 10 people tell you you're a horse, you need to buy a saddle

I needed to buy a saddle.

This wasn't the first time that this had happened to me. At my previous job where I had been in management, I had been told the same thing and friends and colleagues whom I respected had also told me I tended to be too negative.

What stopped me believing what they said?

My own self-representation. The way I saw myself as opposed to the way others saw me.

If somebody had said to me, 'Hey Tim, you're a witty, intelligent and sociable guy' I may have looked slightly embarrassed but inside away from false modesty I would have probably said to myself 'aint that the truth brother!'

When I was told the negative stuff it contradicted my internal picture of myself. Ok, I put my opinions forward a lot but I was a realist not a whiner and businesses needed realists to keep people grounded. So I did what most people do under such circumstances, I got defensive and saw the criticism as a personal attack instead of as valuable feedback and lost the opportunity to use it to develop both as a person and in my career.

How we see ourselves is frequently not how others see us and quite often it's the others that have the better handle on reality.

It takes incredible fortitude to listen patiently while somebody is criticizing you and then sincerely thank him or her afterwards and reflect on the advice. If you can master that skill I guarantee you that people will be commentating on how much you have changed for the better.

Question: How much better could your life be if you could treat criticism as valuable feedback?

7
You Can Do It, You Just Don't Know It.

"I'm always doing that which I can not do, in order that I may learn how to do it."

- Picasso

I frequently get people that I'm coaching telling me that they can't do some particular task or other. The surprising thing is that it's often something that they haven't even tried, or at best, have had only one or two attempts at.

Imagine getting into a car for the first time and declaring "Nope, I just can't seem to get my head round this one I think I'll grab a cab" or somebody else swinging a golf club and when the ball doesn't fly 250 yards down the middle of the fairway claiming that "This isn't right for me I need to check out brain surgery" or another switching on a PC and thinking "Well, this doesn't seem to be computing at all, I think I'll take it back to the store"

Of course all those examples are ridiculous but are they any more ridiculous than somebody claiming that they can't change careers, or learn a foreign language, or quit smoking or even lose 30lbs?

I understand that learning new skills can seem harder as we get older but the operative word there is 'seem'. We get out of the habit of developing our mind but that doesn't mean its ability is in any way inhibited, it just feels that way sometimes. The brain has the capacity up until death to learn new skills and absorb new information if only people would give it the chance.

One method that I use that can be very powerful is the simple use of the word 'yet'. If you can add that three-letter word to every statement claiming that you can't do something you will shift the emphasis completely.

I can't get my handicap under 10 is a statement of fact. I can't get my handicap under 10 yet, is something altogether different. Firstly, it presupposes that you can actually achieve your goal just that you haven't got round to it, and secondly it does something called future pacing. It sends you into the future to a time when you are playing to below 10 and allows you to experience the feelings associated with that, should you so wish.

We are only talking about words here but words are the most powerful tool we have at our disposal. If you can take control of the language you use then you take control of your life and suddenly you can realize that you are a huge resource of untapped potential.

Question: What disempowering beliefs have been holding you back?

8
Change Causes Change

"To improve is to change; to be perfect is to change often"

- Winston Churchill.

One of the things that NLP teaches us is that when we are looking to make changes we need to be aware of the ecological impact of that decision. I'm not talking about flora and fauna but the impact our decision to change has on those around us and indeed ourselves.

Imagine deciding to quit your $250k job because you're stressed all the time, don't like your boss, hate working long hours. You want to follow your natural calling to care for Duckbilled Platypus in the wild. That's all well and good unless of course, you have a large mortgage, kids in school, credit card debt the interest of which could support the State of Delaware and a partner that has a taste for the high life.

Immediately there is a problem looming that you need to be aware of. Yes, there will be many a mortified Duckbilled Platypus when they hear of your dilemma but would you rather let down the cute aquatic egg-laying mammal or your family? That's the problem you have to solve.

The example above is an extreme one but often there are smaller ecological issues that we don't consider. It maybe that you decide to quit smoking and suddenly find yourself gaining weight or you want to get fitter and fail to realize that all the trips to the gym cut down on valuable family time.

I'm not for one moment suggesting that this should stop you setting goals or trying to better yourself. Simply that by knowing up front what other factors could come into play you are much more likely to be able to deal with them effectively and efficiently and not get discouraged and quit.

For more information on ecology in goal setting see Chapter 22.

Question: What potential pitfalls do you need to be aware of when you set goals to improve your life?

9
If He Can – You Can

"The starting point of all achievement is desire. Keep this constantly in mind. Weak desires bring weak results"

- Napoleon Hill

The Sydney to Melbourne ultra-race snakes across Australia's beautiful south east corner covering a distance of almost 550 miles and is considered a real man killer even by seasoned ultra-runners. In 1983 Cliff Young decided to enter. Cliff was not your average athlete; in fact he was not your average anything. Most of the entrants were super fit runners in their prime, whereas Cliff was a 61 year-old cowhand with little competitive experience.

The thing that sets people like Cliff apart from most others is the belief system they adopt. They believe that they set their own rules in life, that the beliefs they hold about themselves actually help them keep going when things get tough rather than causing them to quit, or not even start in the first place. We all have strong beliefs about certain issues it's a fact of life. However, what most of us seldom do is evaluate, and then re-evaluate them to see if they are still relevant. Beliefs are not set in stone, after all, most of us believed in a Santa Claus at some time, but it seems to me that far too many people hold on to beliefs that serve no purpose whatsoever.

Think about some of the beliefs you hold about yourself. Are any of these stopping you achieving your goals through fear of failure or even fear of success? If so, then some work is called for. Break the belief down into bite size chunks and look for examples in your past when you have succeeded at each aspect. If you have achieved something once you can almost certainly do it again. If something is in there that you have never attempted before, look for examples of other people that have succeeded in doing whatever it is and model them. Get advice from experts, read up on the subject, search the Internet, look for a mentor, hire a coach, just do whatever is necessary to obliterate that belief and give yourself a beneficial new one in its place.

It was a hot day in Sydney when Cliff turned up wearing overalls and galoshes over his work boots inviting howls of derision from some of the 150 competitors and growing interest from the press corps. He did not collapse after a few hours or even die as some had predicted; in fact he did rather well. Cliff Young went on to not only finish the 550-mile race, but to win it. Nobody had told him he was supposed to stop for a rest every evening, so he just kept on running whilst others took sleep breaks.

Cliff Young decided what was possible for him, not his family, nor his friends or even society as a whole. He set his parameters in life and he set his own beliefs about what he could and could not achieve.

Question: Do you decide what is possible for you or do you let others decide it for you?

10
Do You Get It?

"Be the change you want to see in the world."

- Gandhi

If you asked me what the key to successful self-development is I would have to say that I think it's taking responsibility for your own life! Everything starts with the act of ownership. Until you take ownership you will forever think of yourself as a victim with no real control over your destiny. The reality couldn't be further from the truth.

I tend to think that the world is split between those that 'get it' and those that don't. Those that 'get it' realize that if they have no money it's because they have not looked after it properly, that if they are overweight it's because they eat too much and don't exercise, that if their relationships always end in disaster that they need to understand what it is they're doing wrong, that if they hate their job they can always leave and that if the dog poops on the carpet it's their own fault for leaving it alone for too long.

Those that 'get it' can change things. They can see problems and deal with them because they know that they alone are responsi-

29

ble for the quality of their lives and as such they are unlikely to sit on their rear end waiting for somebody else to come along and make things better.

People that don't 'get it' can be spotted easier than a giraffe in a tutu riding the subway. They can be heard saying things like "It's my bosses fault", "My wife made me late", "I'd be retired now if it weren't for this Government", "I'm like this because of my parents", "How can I possibly be happy when it's raining" and so on and so forth. They will look for anything to deflect criticism because they know that once they accept responsibility they need to change, and that is obviously not in their nature. They always think it's the world that needs to change.

So ask yourself whether you get it or not. If you do, kudos to you, I applaud you. If you don't, then you are obviously dipping into somebody else's book or you are reading this on autopilot looking for a magic solution to a better life. Let me know if you find it.

Note: I must point out at this stage that taking responsibility never means beating yourself up.

Question: How could your life change for the better if you took total responsibility for it?

11
If You Can Imagine It, You Can Have It

"I visualize things in my mind before I've to do them. It's like having a mental workshop."

- Jack Youngblood

One of the tools I use to help people improve performance is visualization. It's a strange one really because most people that society judges to be successful, such as those that engage in sports already use it on a regular basis. However, when I bring it up in client sessions I nearly always get a strange look. It's as though I've suggested mixing some eye of bat, monkey gland extract and lizard tail and slowly cooking it all over an open fire for 6 hours whilst dancing round naked wearing a Warthog as a hat.

The conscious human mind can only deal with $7 + or - 2$ pieces of information at any one time, therefore, most of the banal day to day stuff is dealt with by your unconscious mind. Think for a moment of all those necessary jobs such as maintaining blood pressure, digesting food, breathing, blinking your eyes, which you do at an unconscious level and without any mindful intervention for the most part. Without your ability to do this you would go into sensory overload and simply be unable to cope with all the information being thrown at you both internally and externally.

The unusual thing about the unconscious mind is that it has a really hard job determining reality from fantasy. It's that ability or drawback (depending on your view point) that allows you to relive events in your mind as though they are happening again. This can be a good thing when recalling pleasurable events but it can be a bad thing when we relive traumatic events with the same intensity, sometimes years after the original event took place.

So what has all this got to do with visualization and success?

Whenever you visualize an event (and by that I mean see what you would see, hear what you would hear, feel what you would feel and being aware of any smells and tastes that maybe associated) you are creating an internal reality that allows your brain to believe it has already lived the event. Now this may or may not be true it really doesn't matter, the only thing that is important is that you see yourself successfully performing a task. As you continually do this in your minds eye it eventually becomes routine so that when you actually need to accomplish a visualized task, the brain says "Ok I know what this is, I know how to do this successfully, so let's do it" You then perform as you'd imagined and desired

Visualization can help you achieve many things. It can help improve performance, reduce nerves, improve memory, accelerate learning and much more. The only real limits are within your own imagination.

Question: Successful athletes and business people know about visualization and embrace it; so presuming you want to be successful, what stops you?

12
Death Is Not The Enemy

"The fear of death follows from the fear of life. A man who lives fully is prepared to die at any time."

- Mark Twain

On the basis of a recommendation from a friend I finally got round to watching "Patch Adams" starring Robin Williams. For those of you that aren't familiar with the movie, it's based on a true story about a guy who, after spending years in a mental institution (he checked himself in after feeling suicidal) decides to leave and train to become a doctor. He wasn't interested in just treating the patients' symptoms and moving on, he wanted to know their names and about their hopes and dreams. He wanted to really connect with them and help improve their quality of life whether they recovered or not. Adams is obviously a remarkable human being.

There was a scene near the end where Adams has to defend his rather eccentric behavior to the University Trustees who at the request of the Dean were considering expelling him. It was a marvelous scene tailor made for a genius like Robin Williams. There was one line that struck me like a freight train and I've played it over and over in my mind since because I think it's so prescient. Not only does it fit perfectly within that scene but I believe that, if used properly, it can have an enormously positive effect on anyone's life and be used as a catalyst to self-development.

"Death is not the enemy"

That may seem a strange phrase to pluck out in isolation and give it such a huge build up, so let me explain why I think it's useful.

We are all going to die. You, me, our families and our friends. In fact in less than 125 years (maybe a bit more if you're very young and exceptionally healthy) there is a good chance that there will be nobody on this earth that ever met you! It's a sobering thought but there's nothing much that we can do about it.

Most people whether they care to admit it or not, are afraid of death. Why is that? Why be afraid of something that happens to millions of people every month? Nobody has ever said it was worse than they expected.

I think the real crux of peoples fear is not that they will die, but that they will die feeling unfulfilled.

If you happen to squeeze every last drop out of a long life, why would you ever fear dying?

On the other hand, if you never quit that job you hate, take the time out for those that you love, visit that country that has always called you, learn to fly, help those in need, join that gym, learn that foreign language or whatever else it is that you know you really passionately want to do, then of course you are going to be scared.

Is there anything in life worse than the feeling that we are not making the most of it, that we are wasting the one and only opportunity we have?

Death really isn't the enemy because we can never defeat it; it's simply (excuse the pun) a fact of life. Look for the real enemies in your life such as inertia, apathy and procrastination and deal with them now so that you have no regrets later.

To the best of my knowledge nobody ever lay on their deathbed and muttered, "At least I got to see the re-runs of "Deal or No Deal" but I suspect millions die wishing they had followed their heart a bit more.

Question: What are the real enemies in your life?

13
Don't Chase Happiness

"Happiness resides not in possessions, and not in gold, happiness dwells in the soul."

- Democritus

There is a line in the United States Constitution with which every person in the country is familiar and it goes:

"We hold these truths to be self-evident, that all men are created equal, that they are endowed by their Creator with certain unalienable Rights, that among these are Life, Liberty and the pursuit of Happiness"

It's the last part that I want to talk about, the pursuit of happiness. Now far be it for me as a Limey to say I think the founding fathers got this bit wrong, but I think the founding fathers got this bit wrong.

I realize that I'm sticking my neck right out there but bear with me here before you hack at it with a rusty scythe; there is an element of method to my madness.

The pursuit of happiness while not necessarily a folly is certainly not something I would encourage you to do. What's that? A Life

Coach not encouraging somebody to be happy? Is he insane or high on a cocktail of bourbon, paint fumes and chest rub? Well, that isn't really what I meant. Of course I want you to be as happy as you can be but also to realize that it's not always possible. When circumstances dictate to the contrary, I don't want you feeling even worse because you are wasting half of your energy trying to remain cheerful and upbeat when there is no need to.

It really is ok to feel down. The truth is you need some lows to experience the highs. If you spend your life trying to fight the inevitable you are going to end up disappointed and dispirited.

Life has huge ups and downs, it was designed that way. No matter who you are you will pass through good times and bad times, happy times and sad times. As adults you're almost certainly going to encounter sickness, frustration, arguments, melancholy, pain, misery and ultimately death. Sorry to be the bringer of bad tidings but most people will be hard pressed to say they feel happy during any of those times.

So if we are not going to pursue happiness, what is the alternative, what do I think it should really say?

Well how about: ...."that among these are Life, Liberty and peace of mind"?

Ok I admit it's not quite as snappy as the original and it needs a bit of work but I like the idea, I think it's got legs.

If you were a Genie and could offer me one wish I would chose peace of mind. Well, maybe world peace or an end to hunger would come first, but if you insisted benevolent Genie that you are that I take something for myself, then peace of mind it is thank you very much.

Imagine if you become ill but you retain your peace of mind, that you lose your job but stay calm internally or of you lost a loved one but could grieve without torturing yourself for all the things that you should have done and said. Wouldn't that be a wonderful thing?

Peace of mind leads to contentment, which in turn leads to a greater chance of happiness. You can't be stressed and have a peaceful mind, you can't be worried or guilty or revengeful or angry or any of the other emotions that do not serve us with peace of mind

The phrase pursuit of happiness indicates that happiness is an external thing and that it's actually always moving away from us, but happiness is internal and it's always with us, if we chose it, and the more peace of mind we have the easier it is to make that choice.

Question: What difference do you think it would make to your life if you pursued peace of mind?

41

14
It's Ok To Feel Down

"I don't think of all the misery but of the beauty that still remains."

- Anne Frank

I was doing a training course one time when I got a text message telling me my soccer team Derby County, had lost a very important game. Twas ever thus!

I think it's fair to say I was upset, maybe not distraught but a close second – a bit like my team had been. I explained to the class what had happened and the significance to me. Then somebody said to me 'You're an NLP Master Practitioner, change your state'

I looked at her and replied 'I don't want to change my state, I like this state thank you very much' There may actually have been another word between 'my' and 'state' for added emphasis but I'll not trouble you with that now.

Sometimes it's ok to feel down or sad on any other 'negative' emotion you care to mention, it's a normal human response to all sorts of different stimuli that happen to us from time to time.

What isn't healthy though, is when you let that feeling persist especially if there is nothing you can do to improve the situation. I wanted to feel miserable and sorry for myself for 10 or 15 minutes so I did. I could have let it drag on and ruined my day but what would that have achieved?

So if you have something in your life that makes you feel really down, that's ok. Simply block out time later on in the day when you can be alone and explore your feelings. Be miserable, be unhappy, cry if it makes you feel better but remember at the end of the time you have allotted yourself to leave all those negative emotions behind, at least until the next time they are needed.

Note: This does not constitute medical advice. If you believe that you may be suffering from a medical condition such as depression, bi-polar disorder, schizophrenia etc please seek appropriate medical help.

Question: How long are you spending feeling bad about things that you can't influence?

15
Know Your Values

"It's not hard to make decisions when you know what your values are."

- Roy Disney

Possibly the single most important thing I do with clients if I want to help them effect lasting change is to understand their values. Without knowing them I often feel like an outsider looking in and understanding their thought processes and motivational drivers is much more difficult.

The thing that seems strange to me is that although these things called values govern what we do, how we do it, how we think, how we interact, and much more, we almost never discuss them. Not only that, but I've never had a client EVER, that knew what his or her values were upfront.

I suppose at this point I should explain what values are and why they are so important. If I asked you what was really important to you in your life and you responded with 'money' then that could be a value, although it's unlikely. So to uncover the real value lurking under the surface the conversation may well go something like this:

'What is important to you about money?

'It allows me to go on vacation when I want'

What is important to you about going on vacation?

'It allows me to relax'

What is important to you about relaxing?

'It allows me to find peace'

What is important to you about peace?

At some stage the client is going to struggle to answer or may even start to loop back on themselves and give the previous answer. This is usually the sign that you are at a core value.

So when I get a list of values, (about 8 is sufficient), I help the client place them in order. I'm not going to go into how I do this here because it requires knowledge of the forms that I use.

So what are the advantages of knowing your values?

If you have any blocks in your life or any areas where you have mixed feelings and are not sure why, they may be caused by a clash of values.

What if you value freedom and family as one and two in terms of importance to you? Then you get an offer for a great job that will give you the freedom to travel the world but will also mean that you are away from you family for half the year. Do you think that would be a problem?

What if integrity is high on your list and you meet a potential partner that has everything you are looking for, they are attractive, witty, fun to be with and whatever else that you want in a partner. Later however, you discover that they have progressed up the corporate ladder by taking credit for other peoples work and they are inherently dishonest. Wouldn't that cause a sense of uneasiness at the very least?

There are also "away from" values that are equally important to us such as poverty, ill health, conflict, hatred, anger, anxiety etc. These are emotions that we will do all we can to avoid and can create the same sorts of blocks as core values. If your number one away from value were stress you probably wouldn't want a job as a politician or an air traffic controller.

The above examples can sometimes be obvious, but not always, the real tricky ones to spot are when the clash of values is internal (within yourself) rather than external (between you and another person or organization etc).

Imagine that you have a number one core value of freedom and a number one away from value of conflict and you want to get divorced and your partner doesn't know it. Do you think you will be able to tell them? Part of you yearns for the freedom and the other part is scared of the conflict it will cause. You could very well end up feeling paralyzed and do nothing.

By knowing that there is a conflict doesn't necessarily mean it will go away but it does make it a lot easier to deal with

Note: I've used words as they relate to me purely for explaining the effect values can have. Freedom may mean something completely different to you than to me, and that's fine. Values are highly personal things and it's important to realize that there is no right or wrong, everyones will be different and should be respected as such.

Question: Do you know what drives you, what motivates you and what inspires you?

16
No News Is Good News

"Bad news goes about in clogs, Good news in stockinged feet".

- Welsh Proverb

I used to be an avid news follower when I lived in the UK. I would listen to the news and news programmes on BBC radio several hours a day and also watch it on TV in the evenings too.

Then a few years ago I started to question what I was doing. I was spending upwards of 3 or 4 hours a day in my car traveling all over the UK and at the end of each day what did I have to show for it? Absolutely nothing other than a good general knowledge on world politics and a few meetings attended. I hadn't learned anything of any importance, I often hadn't laughed at anything and I rarely heard anything positive. That was when I decided to use that time more efficiently and started to buy books on cd.

Now when I was alone in my car I could use the time to my benefit and actually enjoy long drives and not get stressed when stuck in traffic jams. This was fun and after all I could catch up on the news in the evenings if I wanted.

The first week I arrived in the US I had to make a 40-minute drive from where I was living to downtown Orlando. I had a hire car and was listening one of the news channels. During that drive I heard the following: Bird Flu was imminent, Al Queda were planning to attack mainland USA, almost 1 million Americans die each year from heart disease and a story that said if I wasn't worried about kidney disease, then I should be! I felt terrible by the time I reached my destination.

I finally understood when we were in the build up to what looked like becoming Hurricane Ernesto. There was blanket news coverage as you would expect but at the last moment the storm was downgraded and detoured missing central Florida. One of the more popular news stations went to their news crews up and down the coast to get their view. In coaching we often talk about being congruent, i.e. that our words, tonality and body language are all in sync with one another. This was a classic case of lacking any congruence whatsoever as reporter after reporter said the words that it was great news but displayed the body language to suggest that they were disappointed. Ok it was a potential catastrophe but c'mon it was big news, it had people worried and glued to their TV's, there could be journalistic prizes to be had and think of those advertising dollars!

TV news is almost worthless in my opinion. Its stock in trade is misery and fear, it offers little of real value and serves only to bring us all down often just before we go to bed at night. It's easy to catch up on the weather if that is important to you and the Internet allows you to search and find any important stories quickly and easily should you so wish.

I've weaned myself off the news now and I feel better for it. Maybe I'm fooling myself and should really be worrying myself sick about kidney disease but I guess I'll have to learn to live with my naivety.

Question: What does news add to your life?

17
Set Your Own Reality

"There are many ways to be free. One of them is to transcend reality by imagination, as I try to do."

- Anais Nin

I love the topic of reality; it's so subjective that I find it absolutely fascinating. It's one area of our lives where we have complete control and where we decide what is real to us.

Of course society has a habit of imposing limitations on each one of us if we allow it to. The refrains of you're too young, not clever enough, not rich enough etc are heard from a very early age. When somebody wants to act differently from the crowd, to break the rules, to be a bit 'out there' they are frequently ridiculed and derided for their efforts.

Yet without these people there would be no fine art, no scientific breakthroughs, no sportsmen and women pushing themselves to greater and greater feats, no ground breaking music, no cutting edge literature and of course I could go on and on. What our society needs now are more people that think differently, more people that don't care what the rules say, more people striving to be diverse and setting their own parameters.

I was driving down to our local supermarket one time and noticed a couple of people by the side of the road holding signs for condo sales. There was a women and a guy and as this is in an area where permanent signs are not allowed they just kinda stood there, the women reading a book, the guy trying to stay awake. It was a humid day and I could imagine it wasn't a whole heap of fun doing that for 8 hours.

Further down the road there was another sign but this one was moving. On the corner of the intersection just outside the supermarket was a guy dancing! Yep, that's what I said. He was dancing. He was wearing an Ipod or something similar and was twirling his sign, laughing and seemingly having a great time. I couldn't help but smile and think 'good for you'. This looks like a guy that sets his own rules in life, a guy that can take a boring job and turn it into a fun exercise. As well as having a good time I could see he brought fun into the eyes of some of the people that were watching him as they waited at the lights. Not only that, but how much more effective do you think he was in attracting peoples attention to read his sign? 5 times, 10 times? Maybe more? So he was having fun AND being more productive, how cool is that?

I truly believe that this kid will go long way in life. He'll continue to set his own reality and have fun doing so. He may appear weird to some because he isn't prepared to be 'normal' but I'm guessing, and also hoping, he'll not care. I've seen him several times since and every time he is dancing, every time having fun and every time gaining my further respect.

Question: What seemingly boring job could you make fun with a bit of imagination and thus change reality?

18
Stuff Happens

"To enjoy freedom we have to control ourselves"

- Virginia Woolf

I was determined to take it easy and just relax. I had worked every day for 10 straight days and envisioned a day by the pool maybe even with a cold beer and a good book. I like relaxing, it's enjoyable and good for you so why wouldn't anybody do it as much as possible?

I'll tell you why, because of "Stuff", that's why.
Stuff is designed to stop you doing what you really want to do, Stuff expands to fill available time, Stuff arrives when you least expect it and Stuff does its utmost to throw you off track. It has a contract to adhere to because its job is to test you to the limits of your endurance and then just a little bit more. Like a maternal aunt that doesn't realize she outstayed her welcome in 1988, Stuff will hang around ad infinitum if you don't throw it out.

So what is Stuff?
That's a tricky question because it can morph into anything you don't want it to be. It could be a toilet overflowing when you are about to go to the movies, it could be a knock on the door that

ends up being a 30 minute conversation you didn't want, it could be a call to your bank that ends up being 45 minutes long of which 40 minutes is on hold, it could be losing your Internet connection and the phone company saying it's a router fault and the router company saying it's a problem with the phone line. It can be a million different things or just one.

So on this particular day I got hit by Stuff early on and never recovered. I did deal very harshly with some miscreant ants, collect some groceries, write a post for my Blog, mop the floors, clean out my car, cook dinner, and collect a part for the TV but nothing that I'd actually planned to do.

Can Stuff be beaten?
Oh yes, it surely can if only we remember how. Unlike nature, Stuff loves a vacuum. It loves it because it's its job to fill it and fill it quickly. So don't give it chance! Plan out your day, even the ones that do not involve work. If you need 4 hours to chill and relax then write it down in your planner or on your calendar as you would any other appointment, the same goes for the gym, or meditating or even watching TV if that is what helps you relax. Be selfish with your time when you need to be.

This sounds like a lot of trouble and if Stuff never manages to get its talons in you then it may be unnecessary. However, if you are the type of person that gets to the end of the day and wonders where it went and why you didn't get much done. Then you need to act and act quickly.

Question: Is Stuff dominating your life and if so, what do you intend to do about it?

19
Shut The Duck Up

"The more man meditates upon good thoughts, the better will be his world and the world at large."

- Confucius

We all have a voice inside our head that chatters to us constantly about the day-to-day situations we find ourselves in. It's one of the main ways that we interpret external data by constructing conversations internally with ourselves. Although we all have this voice (or more often than not, several different ones) we have our own particular versions some of which can be more helpful than others

Does your voice support and encourage you when things aren't going quite as planned or does it become aggressive, whiny, rude, pessimistic and thinks nothing of tearing a strip off you? Is it often far more hostile and abusive to you than you ever would be to other people?

I once heard this voice likened to that of a bad tempered, miserable, old duck! Yes that's what I said, a duck. Close your eyes and you can hear the voice in your head now quacking away at you. You may not have noticed it's duck-like aquatic qualities before but now you can. Do you know why you can? It's because inside your own head you can hear whatever you want to hear. You can of course hear your own voice in whatever tonality that you care for, or if you'd prefer you could be listening to yourself in the dulcet tones of Jimmy Stewart or James Earl Jones or even Oprah Winfrey. The options are as limitless as your own imagination.

So with all the people to go at, why on earth would anybody ever pick the desperate duck? That's a real tough question to answer. I regularly have people tell me that there isn't any voice inside their head in the first place and I usually respond with "So you're dead then?"

The fact is we have had years to perfect our quacking and it happens so quickly and so unconsciously that many people have stopped noticing it. We mess up at something and the voice is sat there in the background ready to chime in "Quack, you are a failure, you never do anything right, you are an embarrassment" Even when something goes well it can still undermine with "Quack, you just got lucky, wait until they find you out" It's so insidious and so good at its job that its barely noticeable but the overall negative effect on you can be enormous. It has a drip-drip effect that serves over the course of time to make you believe that what it's saying is true, which in turn makes it so. It sets your own reality for you. That's what I said; a duck sets your reality for you.

So maybe it's about time to shut the duck up or at least make him a little bit more friendly and supportive. We do need a voice inside our head so let's pick one that we like. You can drop the duck or whatever you have now and chose a voice that makes you feel good. We still want to be able to get the message across, so don't make it so chilled and laid back that you never take any notice of it. You can even choose 2, 3 or as many voices as you want for different occasions. The only criteria being that the voice should always support you, always be helpful, never aggressive and it never puts you down.

Wouldn't that be great, a voice that treats you with the respect that you deserve, the kind of respect that you like to offer to other people? If you perfect this, and it does need practice to break some embedded habits, then I guarantee you will feel a great deal better about yourself.

Question: What does your duck say to you?

20
Whatever You Do, Just Do Something

"An ounce of action is worth a ton of theory."

- Ralph Waldo Emerson

I was struggling to do some writing shortly after starting my Blog one day. Several times I attempted to start but nothing was forthcoming. So I flicked backwards and forwards checking my e-mails, researching some other work and being on the whole fairly unproductive in the time that I was at my desk.

Writing is important to me in more ways than one. It not only allows me a sense of achievement outside of coaching but it also acts as a cathartic process and one that allows me to assess and clarify my thoughts. Ideas are just ideas when they are inside your head, they come they go, sometimes they get acted on but by and large they simply drift off into the ether often never to be heard from again.

I reckon that I had probably spent well over an hour staring into space when I suddenly remembered a piece of advice I either read or was given many years ago. I forget the source but it was simply this: when you're not sure what to do, just do something.

On the face of it a simple bit of advice but on closer inspection a piece of profound wisdom. In moments of inertia and procrastination that strike us all from time to time the sheer act of doing something breaks the spell, it creates a break state and sends a message to the brain that we are up and running again.

It doesn't matter if what you do is not perfect or that you have to start again or make alterations. Doing nothing, meditation notwithstanding, seldom, if ever, produces the required result. Whereas doing something, at least has the possibility of doing so.

If you're driving along and come to a fork in the road and don't know which way to go and don't have a map, you will eventually choose one way or another. Nobody sits there paralyzed by indecision forever. Yet so many people metaphorically do that with their lives and end up feeling cheated.

So, as I sat there staring at my monitor with that piece of advice echoing in my head I decided to type. I didn't know what it was about or where I would end, I just typed and it felt a whole lot better than staring into space.

Question: What task have you been putting off that if you just started you know would get finished?

21
You Must Read This Chapter

"Watch your thoughts; they become words. Watch your words; they become actions. Watch your actions; they become habits. Watch your habits; they become character. Watch your character; it becomes your destiny."

- Frank Outlaw

There are certain characteristics that are present in a good proportion of people that I see as clients. They very often give themselves a hard time when things are going badly, they have a tendency to procrastinate and more often than not they use language that restricts them and removes choice.

I was in line at a gas station waiting to grab a drink and pay for some fuel. There was a lady in front of me and when it came her time to pay she told the assistant that she needed to get a pack of cigarettes. Wow, I thought, she needs a pack of cigarettes, whatever could be happening that meant she needed them? Was her only son being held ransom by a chain-smoking alligator that demanded 20 Marlboro as a ransom? Or maybe she had undergone some bizarre surgery that had gone tragically wrong meaning that if she didn't get 20 mg's of tar into her lungs every day she'd die? I've no idea what the reason was but I could only presume that it was very serious to warrant such language.

The above may seem silly to you. So what if this lady said she needed a pack of cigarettes, it's no big deal really. Well I happen to disagree; I think it's a very big deal. If you constantly use words and phrases like must, have to, need to and got to, then you gradually remove the choice from your life. Now I'm not suggesting that we shouldn't ever use these words because sometimes they are appropriate but, with excessive use, they send the wrong message to our unconscious mind, a message that says we have no other option or choice here and that we are not even in control anymore.

When I hear clients use these words repeatedly I often stop them at the point they say something like "I have to make $100k this year", and ask the question, "Or what?" It nearly always generates a momentary look of confusion because they have never even considered it before. I must stress that for me to say that I've usually heard several of these phrases (for the interested amongst you they are called model operators of necessity in the NLP field) and can see a pattern forming. If the answer comes back that the client believes her head will fall off, or her house burn down or she will lose her job then fair enough, but more often than not I get a reply along the lines of "Not much" or "I don't really know".

So the next question is this. If you try and retain the element of choice by not bothering to follow through on tasks that you have told yourself repeatedly that you must do, what happens?

You may think that nothing happens (other than the job not getting done) but that's not true. Each time you say that you have to go to the gym or must visit your mother by the weekend or have to lose 25 lbs by Christmas and you don't do it, you have broken a contract with yourself. In isolation there really isn't a problem but if you are doing this repeatedly you are chipping away at your self-esteem until you get to the point where you do not even trust yourself to do anything.

So what can we do to change things for the better? As always the starting point is to observe the words you use. Ask friends and/or family members to mention when you are restricting your own choice and whether your words are appropriate. "I must go to the dentist and get this toothache seen to" is fine. "I need to eat that chocolate cake" is probably not, unless you are on some kind of hyperglycemic rampage. Then simply replace the words such as must, have, need or got to with like, want or would be fun to etc. Immediately you do that it opens up other possibilities and it also makes the undertaking seem less daunting. After all, having to do something is usually less fun than wanting to do it. This takes time and patience so take it easy on yourself and have fun playing about with words.

If and when the woman from the gas station decides to quit smoking my guess is she will have a real tough time of it. She has embedded the message in her unconscious that she needs to smoke. So before she can quit for good she has to break down that particular belief, as well as the addiction, and that probably wont be a whole lot of fun.

69

Question: What unhelpful messages are you sending to your unconscious?

22
Where Are You Going and When Will You Get There?

"If you aim at nothing, you'll hit it every time. "

- Author Unknown

Ok, come with me now, we are going on vacation. Don't worry I've arranged everything all you have to do is turn up. Seriously, that is all you have to do, just make sure you turn up on time. Even you can manage that, surely?

You may want to know when we are going and where, but that's part of the surprise, I can't tell because I don't actually know myself yet. I booked the tickets online and forgot to look where they go to or when they are likely to get there, but hey, that's half the fun, right? So pack your stuffed donkey, the hideous shorts that you only dare wear when you are out of the country, those cheap flip flops, as well as some warm clothing just in case it's a bit nippy and let's go!

I'm guessing you're not coming with me, you seem a bit sheepish. You do realize that this vacation could be an all expenses week of fun in a 5 Star Bali beach hut with free spending money and your own Butler to boot don't you? Ok I admit, it could also be a weekend in a Beirut bed and breakfast, taxi not provided, but we all need some excitement in our lives, that's why we are here, isn't it?

Does the above seem ridiculous to you? Do you think anybody would be so reckless as to book a holiday to an unknown destination for an unknown length of time? I guess a few people would but they are the kind that are already on the edges and probably don't think a third cup of coffee in the morning is pushing the envelope.

I'm going to take a quantum leap here and say as somebody that would not have taken me up on my offer you're probably a sensible, reasonable and practical person. You will not be somebody that leaves things to chance all the time and as such you will have clear written goals of how you are mapping out your life.

What's that? You haven't got written goals?

So how do you know where you are going? More to the point, how will you know when you get there? You have just intimated that you wouldn't get on a plane if you didn't know where it was going but you don't know where your life in general is going.

Wow that's scary, really scary!

At least with a plane ride you can come back after a few hours, ok you may have grossed out on those little pretzel things they give you on planes that don't appear to be on sale anywhere else on the planet and been bored senseless by the garrulous drunk sat next to you, but that is about the worst that can happen, agreed?

What happens if you spend 20 years of your life working your way up the corporate ladder only to find it's leaning against the wrong wall?

It has been proven time and time again that clearly written goals increase the likelihood of them coming to fruition many times over. It's not even close!

If you have things that you desperately want to achieve then write them down clearly, concisely and with as much detail as you can, and do it now. Bring your goals into focus rather than leaving them languishing as some fuzzy vague conception in the nether regions of your mind.

If you want help on goals then either hire a coach or buy a great goal-setting program, but don't walk away from this book without committing yourself to attaining the life of your dreams.

Question: Where are you going?

23
SMARTER Goals

Discipline is the bridge between goals and accomplishment.

- Jim Rohn

As you now know I am very keen on goal setting. I use either an NLP format called "Well-formed Outcomes" or the more traditional SMART goals that is so loved by business coaches. I tend to lean toward the latter simply because I used it a lot when I was in business and it is much easier for clients to use and get familiar with quickly.

Just recently however, I have been getting frustrated with SMART goals because it leaves out a couple of parts that I think are essential to setting great goals. I have been playing about with this in my head for a week or two and came up with my take on SMARTER goals. I say my take because I know that people have had a go at this before. Actually, if the truth is known I didn't know that until I started writing this chapter. I thought I better just do an Internet search before I start making outrageous claims that I am a genius and sheepishly noticed that SMARTER goals got a mere 1.1 million results! The traditional

SMART goals are:

SPECIFIC. So what is it that you want to achieve? Could another person read your goal and know what you were trying to do? If not, then it probably isn't specific enough.

MEASURABLE. Can you measure your goal? If you can't, how do you know where you are with it? If you want to make a certain amount of money, you can always look at your bank balance. If you want to lose 100lbs, you can always check the scales to see where you are. However, if you want to be wealthy, how do you know when you get there, how do you measure how close you are to attaining the goal? The simple answer is you can't, it is immeasurable.

ACTION ORIENTED. This is a real bugbear of mine and if I see this listed as "Achievable" one more time I will scream. Honestly I will, just try me. It is NOT achievable or attainable because they are the same as R, which we will cover next. You cannot have a goal that doesn't require you to do anything, you have to get off your rear end and actually do something. Sitting in a comfy chair and hoping the mailman will deliver you a check for a million bucks is not a goal it is a hope or a dream. By the way, some publications do use "Agreed Upon" here and whereas I am more ok with that than achievable I still prefer "Action Oriented"

REALISTIC. Now do you see why we don't need achievable? They are effectively the same thing. I am not that keen on realistic because some of the greatest achievements were unrealistic. I would rather you set a goal of earning $1m this year and get to $850k than aim for $250k and hit it. Goals can be moved and adjusted but the rule of thumb is aim high. Realism is for accountants.

TIMEBOUND. For those of you that have ever worked in sales you will know that the one thing that kills more deals (that appear to be going well) than anything else is the time element. If there is no time limitation then deals don't get done because there is always something more urgent for prospects to attend to. The same applies to goals. If you set a goal of losing 20lbs with no time limit then you have given yourself carte blanche to do nothing because next week will always do. Set a deadline and stick to it.

So there you have the traditional SMART goals outline but now I would like to add two more to make them SMARTER.

ECOLOGICAL. I am not talking about global warming here or saving cuddly jungle life from farmers on slashing and burning rampages. I mean that external factors need to be taken into consideration. If you have a goal to live in Mongolia and raise Mountain Goats and your spouse/parents are delightfully happy where they are thank you very much, then you need to take that into consideration. Of course you may still want to go and don your furry hat and curly shoes but you may need to leave the rest of the family behind. There is a more serious message to all this. What if you have a goal to quit smoking and then find that the only time you ever get to leave the office for 10 minutes and free your mind is when you go outside to have a cigarette? That could be problematic. That is not to suggest that you give up on a worthy goal more that you look for other ways to achieve whatever it is you may lose.

REWARD. So what is it you want? What is the reward? What will you see, hear and feel when you get to your goal? You may have a goal of earning $1m but what is the real reward behind that? That money is useless in isolation, so what does it REALLY get you. Look past the obvious, drill down and keep asking, "So what else does that get me?" When you can go no further then that is the real reward; that is the pay off that will motivate you if things get tough.

I noticed when trawling the web after I had done this that somebody else had used the E to stand for enthusiastic. Well that is cool, I understand that enthusiasm will help but it is not a necessity in my humble opinion. I often set short-term goals for things that I hate doing but know that I need to do. Enthusiasm is definitely not something that is dripping out of every pore when I start although sometimes I wish it were.

*Question: **What is the real reward you are looking for from your life?***

24
Don't Take This Personally

"I care not what others think of what I do, but I care very much about what I think of what I do! That is character!"

- Theodore Roosevelt

I'm sorry to say this but you are a complete imbecile. I know you probably don't like hearing it but the truth will out and that's just the way it's so you may as well accept it

I'd also like to tell you that you are too fat or too thin, your hair is a mess, you're no fun to be around and nobody likes you!

If any of this fits your internal picture of yourself and you are apt to listen to the opinions of others you may well be thinking 'How does he know all this stuff, is he a mind reader?' On the other hand if it doesn't fit your own perception or you don't care what I think you're probably wondering "What a jerk, he needs locking up for his own good"

Well of course I'm joking, I would never insult anybody astute enough to be reading a book of mine, there simply aren't enough of you around.

There are about 6 billion people on this planet and about 5,999,999,000 of them don't know you and probably don't want to know you. Of the people that do know you probably less than 10% know you very well and of that 10% nobody comes even close to knowing you as well as you do. Yet even bearing in mind all those figures literally millions of people every day allow their mood to be dictated by other peoples opinions, gestures, actions and the meanings both accurate and more often inaccurate that they attach to them. Now that's what I call a run on sentence!

If that women you barely know gives you a strange look at work one day she might indeed be doing it because she dislikes you or she may be having a bad day and hasn't even noticed you. How about the driver that cuts you off on the Freeway, yes he may of course be trying to kill you, but it's more likely he's simply in a hurry or distracted by his cell phone. The boss shouting at you could mean that you are about to be fired or it could mean he's just found a nasty little rash and he wants to take it out on you. Not that the rash, his anger that is.

The point of this is twofold: Firstly you can never know exactly what is going through somebody else's mind. It's difficult enough to know what's happening in your own head never mind anyone else's so there's a good chance that any assumptions you make will be erroneous. So why bother trying?

Secondly, even if they were thinking something negative about you, why would you care? Do you really worry what a casual acquaintance thinks about you? Why would you even value the opinion of someone that's prepared to judge so easily?

If you've given somebody a genuine reason to think badly of you then I understand you may want to make reparation. Other than that, the only sensible course of action is not to allow the opinions of others to dictate what you think about yourself. The alternative is to give all your personal power away and spend you entire life in a fruitless attempt to please other people.

Don't seek the approval of others, seek the approval of yourself and let others follow if they wish.

Question: How often do you presume you know what somebody is thinking even when they haven't told you?

25
Do What You Love.

"A tremendous number of people in America work very hard at something that bores them. Even a rich man thinks he has to go down to the office everyday. Not because he likes it but because he can't think of anything else to do."

- W H Auden

Do you like your job or maybe even love it? Do you get out of bed in a morning with a spring in your step, a smile on your face and eagerly looking forward to the day ahead? Does it invigorate and thrill you, motivate and engage you? Would you do whatever it is for free, if you didn't need the money? Do you gush to friends about it and want to talk 'shop', and by that, I do not mean whining about an unfair boss or poor pay.

My guess is that if you are anything like the people I speak to on a daily basis, the answer to most, if not all of those questions, is a resounding and unambiguous NO!

So why do you do it? Is it for the money? Is it because you are close to retirement and are just hanging in there? Is it for security? Is it because you don't know what else to do? Is it because you don't think anybody else will hire you? Is it because you are fearful of telling your spouse you want to change careers at age 40?

The average person spends approximately half their waking life between the ages of 20 and 65 at work. Based on a low average (at least in the USA) of 40 hours per week and assuming a generous vacation time of 5 weeks per year that is 84,600 hours potentially doing something they don't like!

Why would anybody do that?

The most common answers I get to that question are listed above, but sometimes I get even more bizarre reasons such as 'My parents always wanted me to do this' or 'I came here part time 25 years ago and never left'. Well there's a great career plan!

Let me make a contentious statement. If you are in a job that you hate, have always hated and will always hate, then you should leave and leave as quickly as you can. Life is way too short to spend so much time being unhappy or unfulfilled.

What would you like to do more than anything else? Think about that for a moment, really seriously think about it. If I'm Merlin the Magician and I can give you any job, what would it be?

How about the CEO of a large blue-chip multi-national corporation with thousands of people under your control? Or how about a world-class athlete, or a famous musician or artist? What about becoming a teacher, or a gardener or a nurse or perhaps a writer?

Whatever your answer to the above, there is a reason why you want to do whatever it is, and that is because you think it will make you happy.

That's all that most of us want, to be happy.

So what makes you happy? What already gets you in the zone and motivated? Could you get anybody to pay you to do that? Could you set up a business doing whatever it is? If it's yes to either of those questions, then what are you waiting for? If it's no, then look harder, you are missing something!

A few years ago my niece approached me at her 21st birthday party and asked me if I would help coach her in sales. I was amazed that she wanted to stay in sales after just leaving University with a degree in Criminology, but she patiently explained that it was potentially good money in the telemarketing call center where she worked part-time, even though she hated it.

We chatted for a while and I told her why I thought it wasn't right for her (which she already knew deep down) and then asked her what she really loved to do. Ski and party was the response. '"Well get somebody to pay you to do that'" I replied. Not unexpectedly, she rolled her eyes. But we chatted some more and discussed what opportunities there may be.

The result was that she got a job with a leading vacation company that offered exactly the kind of opportunity that she was looking for. In the winter she became a ski guide and chalet hostess at a top Alpine resort. Then in the summer she worked as a tour guide on a Greek island. Admittedly, the money wasn't great and she had to work hard, but she had a lot more fun than if she had gone into sales, no matter how much money she would have earned. Best of all, she was happy!

Always believe that there is a way to find your passion, because if you always believe it's just around the corner then you wont miss it when it's staring you in the face. If and when you start to believe it's not possible, then guess what? It isn't.

People make money doing all sorts of weird and wonderful things, things that they genuinely love. People actually get paid to go shopping, eat food, tell jokes, play with toys, design things, play sports, pretend they are other people, write stuff, daydream, drive cars, care for animals, fly planes, talk, coach people and more or less anything else you can imagine.

I can't guarantee that you will earn big bucks living your dream but if you are really happy and can meet your basic needs do you really care? If you are doing something you are passionate about how much more likely are you to be hugely successful than when you were doing work you hated anyway?

Question: What do you truly love to do, and how can you make money from it?

26

Don't Let Fear Hold You Back

"He who has conquered doubt and fear has conquered failure"

- James Allen

A while ago I was working with a client and he mentioned the word fear. I asked if he's heard of the acronym sometimes used to describe this word that seldom offers us anything beneficial and more often serves only to hold us back. He hadn't, but before we go there, ask yourself whether you suffer from any of the following fears:

Fear of change

Fear of being too old or too young

Fear of stepping outside your comfort zone

Fear of poverty

Fear of being too fat, too thin, too tall, too small

Fear of failure

Fear of illness

Fear of fear

Fear of reading any more self-help books that talk about fear

I doubt you can say that you don't suffer from any of the above but if you can, congratulations, you've really got life in perspective, you may as well put the book down and go and bask in the glow of sweet success. If not you had better carry on reading.

Fear, like its cousin worry, is one of those emotions that never really serve us. Thousands of years ago we needed fear as we hunted, gathered and generally tip toed around the forbidding landscape trying to avoid saber toothed tigers and any other malevolent beasties intent on making us lunch. That was then and this is now.

Fear can be useful. After all, horror films wouldn't be very successful without being able to generate fear nor would a 400-foot drop on a roller coaster ride. Similarly, we still do need fear to stop us running across an Interstate dressed only in flippers and a sombrero otherwise we might indeed get arrested and/or run over. On the whole though fear is something that tends to slow us down or very often hold us back completely.

The other thing about fear is that it's frequently misplaced. We are often fearful when we don't need to be about situations that are either not very important in the great scheme of things or simply do not represent real danger. An exam does not represent danger, nor does a job interview or that roller coaster ride. Rarely is there any real need to fear a plane ride, snakes and spiders are primarily non-threatening to humans and that creak in the house at night probably isn't an axe-wielding maniac. I could go on and on and usually I do, but I suspect you get the message.

Next time you are fearful of something ask yourself this question. Are my fears based in common sense and if so do I need to act accordingly, or is my fear really False Evidence Appearing Real? Look closely at the circumstances and see if you are over-estimating the odds of danger, do not let the fear run amok (unless you like that kind of thing, in which case knock yourself out) without understanding your true situation in an objective and logical way. Is the evidence you have to hand, true, false or in any doubt whatsoever? Are there counter examples of where you've easily coped with such a position or where there was shown to be no genuine danger in the final outcome?

A little bit of fear can help us perform better and give us an edge, but when it becomes paralyzing it's time to do something about it. There is nothing as efficient as fear for preventing people from achieving their true potential in life and paradoxically that is something that really is worth being fearful about.

Question: What fears are holding you back from achieving your full potential?

27

Bite Your Lip

*"Men who know little say much, men who know much
say little".*

- Unknown

I was lying in bed one night pondering a conversation I'd had
with a friend earlier that day. It had been a lively discussion
about the corporate world and I was fairly opinionated about
what I thought made an honest and ethical company.

My friend pointed out that I had a blind spot about certain
things and to be honest this made me a little defensive.
Immediately my mind began searching for examples where he
had displayed similar behavior. I felt the need to prove that he
was just as bad, probably even worse, than me in this regard! I
think it's fair to say I didn't hear all he was trying to say because
I was already composing my own dastardly cunning response!

One of the first questions I ask people when they come for life
coaching is what is the minimum they want to achieve that will
make their investment in time and money worthwhile. I like
this question because it achieves two goals. For the client it asks
them to think about what is important to them at that point in

time and for me it helps me identify the path I need to take to help them achieve their objective. If we have no end game in mind when we set off to, no goals or targets, how do we define success? It's a little like hailing a taxi with no idea where you want the driver to take you.

My friend knew me quite well and he asked me to not say anything until I had thought about what he'd said for a while. Five years ago I doubt I would have even drawn breath before diving back in or storming off in a self-indulgent huff, but I'm pleased to say I managed to bite my lip and keep quiet.

After a night of reflection did my opinion change? Maybe a little bit, but that isn't really the point. What changed was the way I viewed the conversation, I no longer felt compelled to batter my point home and recognized that my friends' opinion was as valid as mine.

So next time you are in a similarly heated situation quickly ask yourself

'What do I want to gain from this?'

If the answer is that you want to make the other person feel small, to learn nothing, to create a hostile atmosphere and to be thought of as arrogant then go ahead and win that sucker, if win is the right word!

On the other hand, if you would like to exit feeling good about yourself, learning a bit more about somebody else and what makes them tick and leaving them with a favorable opinion of you, back off and listen. Try and understand what they are saying and then respect their opinion as you do your own because, and here's the deal, if you had been born with their genes, had their upbringing and lived in their shoes you would indeed have their opinions.

Question: What could being quiet and listening more often achieve for you?

28

Curiosity Didn't Kill The Cat

"Be curious always! For knowledge will not acquire you; you must acquire it."

- Sudie Beck

Can you remember when you were a little kid how curious you were about the world? You would ask questions like why is the sea blue, where does the sun go at night, where did I come from and why is that doggy climbing on top of that other doggy?

At that age we learn so much and so quickly that it seems almost inconceivable to us now. Why do you think that is? Our brains are no more able to learn at 2 than they are at 82 but something changes.

Could it be that our curiosity diminishes? Does that fresh-faced eagerness to learn and understand gradually get replaced by cynicism and a belief that we know pretty much all we need to know?

Kids learn because they ask questions because they are fascinated by life and all that's around them, but that curiosity and thirst for knowledge has often been destroyed by the time they hit 5th grade.

Have you ever heard an adult, be they parent, schoolteacher or just a well-meaning friend say to a child 'stop asking stupid questions'? What they don't realize because they have lost their own sense of wonder is that there are no stupid questions if they are coming from a genuine desire to learn. There are stupid responses like that one though. The same holds true when kids are told to 'be quiet' or to simply 'do what you are told and don't ask why'? What message does that send to them during a period of their lives when they are so impressionable? Maybe it tells them that it doesn't pay to be inquisitive that it's best to keep your head down, go with the flow and be like everybody else?

Be more curious, don't accept things at face value, ask dumbass questions and most of all encourage others, especially kids, to do the same. There is no age limit on learning and we have the ability to do it until the day we die, don't waste that opportunity.

Question: Have you tamed your natural inclination to be curious? If so, what can you do to regain it?

29
Control Your Thoughts

To enjoy good health, to bring true happiness to one's family, to bring peace to all, one must first discipline and control one's own mind. If a man can control his mind he can find the way to Enlightenment, and all wisdom and virtue will naturally come to him.

- Buddha

A number of years ago I was playing golf with a friend back in the UK and as was often the case, talk turned to work. We'd met working for the same company and he had progressed up the corporate ladder faster than a frog leaving a blender manufacturers conference.

I was less than complimentary about the company and quite frankly was ripping them mercilessly when suddenly I said:

"You do realize that they don't give a damn about you or their customers, they only care about profits and growth"

He looked at me, laughed and then sad:

"That may or may not be true but I simply can't let that thought into my head. If I did, I wouldn't be able to perform like I do now"

At the time I didn't get it at all. In fact my respect for him was somewhat diminished because I saw him as somebody who was burying his head in the sand rather than face up to his ethical and moral responsibilities.

Now when I think of that conversation I view it in a very different light. Maybe he didn't accept ethical and moral responsibility for a multi-billion pound business but why on earth should he?

What he did was to accept total responsibility for the thoughts inside his head; those that served him and those that held him back. That's a skill few of us possess.

Of course he could have resigned and left the business galloping away on the high moral horse that I had lent him. Or he could have stayed and tried to change things for the better from the inside. I'm glad to say he took the latter option.

Question: How would your life be better if you controlled what you thought about?

30
Don't Control Your Thoughts

"If you don't control your mind, someone else will"

- John Allston

Ok, so I know I'm now doing a complete volte-face and contradicting what I just wrote about controlling your thoughts but I'm allowed to do that because it's my book.

I sincerely believe that you need to be aware of what you are thinking especially all that nasty insidious stuff that can make you feel miserable and drag you down but I also think that you sometimes need to let your thoughts run wild.

If you've ever had the fun of working with a group of creative people you'll know what I mean when I say they can be unpredictable at best and close to sheer lunacy at worst. There are no bad ideas in that kind of environment, just ideas that haven't yet been fine-tuned or have not found their niche in life. You never hear people shouted down for something that on the surface seems preposterous. That's because they know that computers were once ridiculous as were MRI's, mass-produced cars and they are some of the saner ideas. Imagine being the person that had to stand up and sell pet rocks or hoola hoops to a board of directors!

Creativity is to some extent a gift but it's also something that you can work at. If you've been brought up in an atmosphere where unusual opinions were frowned upon or even worse, ridiculed, then you may well have 'learned' to bottle up your creative juices.

Well how about uncorking them again?

Wouldn't it be great to have a stream of ideas flowing through your consciousness just waiting to be plucked from obscurity and used to make your life better?

So here's the deal. Grab yourself 30 minutes and prepare to relax, if you can't manage 30 minutes, 20 will do and if you can't spare 20 minutes what the heck are you doing reading this book? Get back to work now!

I'm not going to tell you how to relax as there are a number of different ways and what ever is best for you is best for you. I really like progressive relaxation for this process. This involves relaxing each muscles group in turn starting at either the top and working down or at the bottom and working up and going through the entire body. Once you have done this send a wave of relaxation through you body and check for any areas that you may have missed the first time.

When you are completely chilled to the bone simply let your mind wander. Observe your thoughts but do not judge them. It may help to keep a journal handy so that when that earth-shattering idea makes it's way into your mind you can write it down before it heads for the exit again. Don't worry you can always relax again if you wish but c'mon how many brilliant ideas do you expect from each session? You're getting this for free you know!

That is about as complicated as any of this gets. Don't force anything, simply lie there and see what happens when you let your creative unconscious have a bit more freedom to run riot. You can if you prefer do the same thing nodding off at night as long as you keep the journal handy. I can't tell you how many ideas that I've had that I just knew were going to make me a million bucks last thing at night only to find that they'd sneaked off into the nether reaches of my mind by morning never to be heard from again. I'm sure I invented flip flops and the Internet as well as discovering superstring theory and that was just one Saturday night a few years ago after a few beers, so heaven knows what else I've done and forgotten about.

Question: How could unlocking your untapped creative potential help you?

31
Embrace Failure

"To begin to think with purpose, is to enter the ranks of those strong ones who only recognize failure as one of the pathways to attainment."

- James Allen

Do you go out of your way to avoid disappointment and letdown in your business and home life? Do you ever back away from projects that you think are risky and do not guarantee success? Do you steer clear of situations where you feel like a fish out of water because you don't enjoy the feeling of not being in control? Do you see people that mess up or fall short in something as being failures in life?

Richard Branson has constantly taken risks both in his private and business lives and many of his businesses have been less than successful, yet he is quite rightly seen as an icon in the business world. Donald Trump declared business bankruptcy in the early 90's and almost had to declare personal bankruptcy the following year but he does ok for himself. Not many people either side of the Atlantic would really think of either Branson or Trump as failures yet they have failed.

The most effective and successful people in life are risk takers and do you know why that is?

They know that the more you fail the more you learn, that the more you learn the more you succeed and therefore the more you fail the more you succeed.

As humans we learn much more quickly by failing at things and noticing what doesn't work. As babies we learn to walk by putting one foot in front of the other and just trying it out. When we fall over we do not think 'huh, I guess I've not got this walking thing right at all, I guess I'll stick to crawling'. No, we get back up and try again, we have not learned to be embarrassed by failure at that age so we tenaciously keep going. Not only that, but we are encouraged by our parents when we do well and just as pertinently, not rebuked for falling over.

Then something strange starts to happen. As we go through the school years suddenly it becomes apparent that failing is no longer quite such an acceptable option. Sports teams are pushed hard to succeed by coaches, mom and dad want to see straight A's on that report card, teachers use red pen to highlight your errors and the smallest indiscretion can result in raucous laughter and finger-pointing by peers.

So bit-by-bit we withdraw into our shell and start to develop the fear of failure that is so prevalent in our society. We are actually taught this by parents, teachers, peers, family members etc, it wasn't hard wired in before birth. Of course nobody really means to do this, most of the advice and admonishments are well meaning but the damage is done nevertheless.

To be really successful in life we need to embrace failure and not fear it. We need to approach projects with an attitude that says 'I'll do my best and if that doesn't work, no problem I'll try something new'. We are human beings we mess up, but if we can laugh at and learn quickly from our mistakes we remove the need to worry about failure, as well as making it much less likely to happen in the first place.

Question: What can you fail at a bit more often to get you to where you really want to be?

32
Belief Is A Powerful Thing

*"Believe nothing just because a so-called wise person said it.
Believe nothing just because a belief is generally held. Believe
nothing just because it's said in ancient books. Believe nothing
just because it's said to be of divine origin. Believe nothing just
because someone else believes it. Believe only what you yourself
test and judge to be true."*

- Buddha

There is a tribe of Indians living in Mexico called the
Tarahumara that leave me in awe every time I hear mention of
them. They can run like no other people on earth often doing so
for 100 miles at a time with ease and without any of the injuries
you would associate with such incredible accomplishments.

I once heard a story and it may very well be apocryphal.
Apparently, one member of their tribe was persuaded to run in
a marathon race in the US. The sponsor of the Indian was convinced that he would win easily as this was only a sprint to him.
So he arranged to have him flown to the US and was very excited
about the prospect of this unknown man making them both
famous. Alas, the Tarahumara Indian came in well down the

field and when challenged about his poor performance explained that he thought he was still on the warm up!

Are these people genetically different to us in the West? No not really. They may well have slightly improved lung capacity and a higher red blood cell count to help oxygenate their blood but nothing that would come even close to explaining their abilities...except maybe one thing.

They grow up to believe that they can run prodigious distances, and that it's normal and well within their abilities. Whereas we grow up to believe that people that run marathons in less than 3 hours are almost super-human. It seems reasonable to expect then that both sets of people will prove themselves right.

So on reflection maybe they do have an unfair advantage because their society didn't tell them they should be more realistic and that they can't do that because it simply isn't possible.

Question: What could you do if only you believed you could?

33
Ask For Help

"It's one of the most beautiful compensations of this life that no man can sincerely try to help another without helping himself."

Ralph Waldo Emerson

My sister and brother-in-law came to stay with us not long after we moved to Florida and they hired a car to drive down to the Florida Keys for a few days. When they returned the car it had an added feature...their binoculars. They weren't even missed until they unpacked when they got home.

A few days later I got an unexpected call from the car rental company advising me the binoculars had been found. Unfortunately we live about 40 minutes away from the rental return so I said I would pick them up when I was next in the vicinity. I stopped by twice and whilst the office was open the lost property department was closed. Once was my fault because it was Saturday and I should have realized there would be nobody there but the other time was midweek just after 4.00pm and I only missed them by a minute or two as they had closed on the dot at 4.00pm

The lady that originally phoned to tell me they had been found called two or three times more but we kept missing each other. When she did finally get hold of me she explained that they were only allowed to keep items for 30 days and that my time was up. She couldn't keep them stored any longer as they were due an inventory.

My week was fully scheduled and I knew I wouldn't be able to make it over before her deadline so I tried to persuade her to work with me. We talked for about 2 or 3 minutes with no resolution in sight when I changed tack and asked for help. I simply said 'Is there anyway you can help me resolve this situation because I simply can't get to you before next week?'

That one sentence created a quantum shift in the ladies attitude to me. She went from being efficient and curt to trying to come up with all sorts of creative ideas. Eventually and without me really saying anything more she said 'I'll tell you what, I'll make an exception in this case and put them to one side until next week' I thanked her profusely and hung up.

People on the whole like to lend a hand, we like to feel needed it makes us feel good. How often do you stop somebody for directions and they refuse help? Maybe every once in a while or if you are in a large city but on the whole people love to help. Too often in life we battle away on our own because that's the way we have always done it, when a simple request for help will not only make us feel better but give somebody else the chance to feel better about themselves too. Now that is what I call a win/win situation.

Question: Who can help you if you just asked them to?

34
Your Best Is Always Good Enough

"Always Do Your Best. Your best is going to change from moment to moment; it will be different when you are healthy as opposed to sick. Under any circumstance, simply do your best, and you will avoid self-judgment, self-abuse and regret."

- Don Miguel Ruiz

I was reading on the Internet about some guy that had been trying to break his personal best for running a 10k race. It was an unremarkable story except for one quote that stood out and made me do a double take.

'I guess my best wasn't good enough.'

What was going through this guy's head when he was thinking that his best wasn't good enough? Good enough for whom? Himself? His peers? His parents? The Dalai Lama?

I started to think about all the times when I've heard people say similar things, either to others or about themselves, and it made me feel a little bit sad. I remembered hearing schoolteachers say it to pupils and coaches say it to athletes and even me saying it to myself many years ago.

My best simply wasn't good enough.

Even as I'm writing this I can't help but envision the sigh and the slumping of the shoulders of the person that receives such information even if it's from themselves.

How do we measure good enough?

If it was a goal of somebody's it certainly wouldn't classify as a SMART goal because it isn't specific, measurable, action oriented or time bound. I guess it could be realistic but we don't really have enough information so it pretty much misses every criterion.

Every day you get up and move about the world with two options. You can do the best you possibly can in every endeavor whether that's looking after a child, going to work, playing sports or whatever else you do each day. Or you can drift along half-heartedly. There really are no other options, there is no best and a bit more, there is no 110% (no matter what you hear athletes being interviewed for TV saying) or better than best.

You can only ever do your best.

So bearing that in mind why on earth would we ever tell anybody their best wasn't good enough when it's all any of us have to offer? More importantly, why would we ever say it to ourselves?

I understand that sometimes trying your best doesn't guarantee that you get that job, win that race, attract that partner etc, but so what? Giving your best is victory in its own right. If you ever feel like you've done that but still not won the prize, pat yourself on the back nevertheless, and accept that it was a job well done.

Question: What could you view differently by accepting that your best is always good enough?

35
You Get What You Focus On

"Only one thing has to change for us to know happiness in our lives: where we focus our attention."

- Greg Anderson

I never get ill. Seriously, I don't think I've had more than 2 or 3 days off work in the last 10 years and it's something that I'm rightly or wrongly proud of. This doesn't mean I suffer through illness and carry on, it means I simply never feel run down.

I thoroughly believe that you get what you focus your attention on in life, and that we become the product of our thoughts. I'm not sure whether this is scientific fact i.e. like attracts like and that's just physics or whether it's more esoteric than that, and to be honest I'm not sure I really care.

I had a conversation about this with my mother-in-law when I was on vacation as she has had numerous health problems over the last few years. I pointed out rather smugly, that I didn't get ill and that I seldom even thought about it and never expected it in the way she seemed to and suggested she just change the focus of her attention?

Then the day after we got home from our vacation I got really sick. This wasn't a cold it was proper flu with the associated dizziness, aching limbs, blurred vision and hot and cold sweats. I was laid low in bed for 4 days and didn't do much of anything for over a week.

A week or so after I recovered I had to travel back to the UK for a few days. I must admit that I don't like long haul flights but endure them nevertheless as a necessary evil. When I was there I went to see some friends who have 2 kids, both of whom had been ill. You've guessed it; within two days I was feeling several degrees under resulting in a miserable flight home.

On reflection I think I should start to take my own advice more often. The minute I started to talk about being ill when I was on vacation my attention shifted to thinking about it and even wondering why I appeared to be so immune from general cold and flu viruses the majority of the time, even when they are in my own family. Then when I heard my friend's children had been ill once again I started to think about it and even expect that I would end up suffering on my flight home. So I did!

Is all this a coincidence? I guess it could be but I tend to think not and as changing my thinking back to how it was prior to going away costs nothing, then I'm prepared to embrace that belief again. I encourage you to try it out for a few months; after all, what have you got to lose?

Note: I would like to point out that I'm not suggesting that all illness is self-imposed, just that there is no harm in keeping an open mind to helping ourselves out whenever we can.

Question: What are you focusing your attention on?

36
Turn Off Your Phone And Relax

"One of the symptoms of an approaching nervous breakdown is the belief that one's work is terribly important."

- Bertrand Russell

I was at the gym one time and got on the treadmill next to a woman who was probably in her mid to late twenties. Almost immediately she made a phone call and started chatting to a friend about (it seemed to me) nothing in particular. Within a minute or so a middle aged guy got on the cross trainer the other side of me and also made a call. He was obviously making a business call and was talking very loudly. In fact he was so animated that I expected him to either fall off or have a seizure and I idly wondered whether the gym carried a defibrillator for such emergencies. Both calls went on for in excess of 15 minutes without any medical calamities and I was glad that I had my Ipod to drown out the background noise.

The following day I had a dental appointment and there were 2 other people in the waiting room at the same time as me. One guy was on a laptop and talking into a cell phone and the other was just talking on a cell phone. Unfortunately, I didn't have my Ipod with me and sat there in the crossfire of two competing conversations looking forward to the relative peace and quiet of a nice drill and suction machine.

Are our lives really so hectic now that we can't either exercise or go to the dentist without having a cell phone or laptop for company? Will business grind to a halt and our social lives cease to exist unless we're available 24/7? If so, how did we cope as little as 10 years ago when cell phones were a rarity? Are our lives so much better now for this seemingly eternal connectivity?

Next time you are tempted to take your phone into the gym, the dentists office or anywhere else for that matter where it's not completely appropriate, ask yourself whether it's absolutely necessary. If it is (and I accept for some people that may occasionally be the case), then go ahead and take it, if not, stick it on silent or leave it in the car or at home. You'll be able to see who has called and people can leave messages if it's really important.

Am I being a killjoy about this and do I need to develop a little more tolerance and patience? Well I'm happy to let you decide. Sometimes we need to give ourselves a break to get away from the hurly burly of life, not to mention those around us, whether that's in the gym where we can zone out or even for 10 minutes reflecting in the dentists office, it really doesn't matter. Trust me when I say, your world will almost certainly not collapse and more importantly, your conscious mind will thank you for giving it some time off with improved performance and a reduction in stress levels.

Question: What opportunities is life offering you to give your mind vital down time that you are missing?

37

Had A Bad Day – How Do You Know?

"We know what we are, but know not what we may be"

- William Shakespeare

A farmer had small plot of land, and if he worked day and night 7 days a week with his son there would be just enough food for him and his family to exist on. One day his only horse ran away. A neighbor heard the terrible news and went round to comfort him.

"I've heard about your horse running away and that is terrible news"

"No it isn't?" said the farmer.

"What do you mean said his friend I know how hard you work with that horse, that without it you can't feed your family, that is just terrible'

"Ah" said the farmer "But what you don't know is that the horse came back, and not only did it come back, but it brought two other horse with it, I've got 3 of them now!"

"Wow" said the neighbor "That is fantastic news."

"No it isn't" said the farmer!

"'What do you mean?" said the neighbor "You have 3 horses it will be easier, you will have more food, more spare time, I don't get it"

"Well what you don't know" said the farmer "Is that my son tried to tame one of the horses, got thrown off and broke both his legs, now he can't help me'"

"Oh my goodness, that's terrible news' said the neighbor"

"'No it isn't" said the farmer

"Wait a minute" said the neighbor "How can that not be a catastrophe to you and your family, you need your son?"

"Because today the militia came by and recruited all the able bodied men and skipped my son because of his broken legs" said the farmer

"That's fantastic news" said the neighbor.

"No it isn't" said the farmer'

That story goes on ad infinitum as you can imagine. What it demonstrates is perspective. Seldom do we know when an event happens what will be the long-term implications. A job firing could lead to a better career or finally working for yourself. A long line in the post office when you are late for an appointment may mean you speak to somebody that alters the course of your life for the better. A traffic jam on the Interstate may cause you to tune into a radio show that you wouldn't normally listen to resulting in some information that leads to a breakthrough in your life. A bankruptcy may cause you to reassess and start again with experience that you couldn't buy with any amount of money and so on and so forth.

Of course you could presume that every unplanned event or temporary crisis is terrible news and work hard on developing that ulcer. Or you could simply smile and presume that everything is as it's meant to be and even 'bad days' often turn out for the best in the fullness of time.

Question: How would suspending judgment at the end of a 'bad' day improve your mood?

38
Manifest The Best

"We attract into our experience that, and only that, which we think about – whether wanted or unwanted"

- The Law Of Attraction

I have spoken about some of the more esoteric stuff that I do as a life coach and made mention of manifesting and I'd like to talk a little bit more about that because it's such an interesting field.

Stay with me on this one if you are unfamiliar with it because it's an easy concept to grasp but a tricky one to embrace for a lot of people.

For thousands of years certain cultures have believed that it was possible to attain the life of your dreams through the power of the mine or as Wayne Dyer puts it, the power of intention. To most people in modern society who have been brought up to believe that the only way you get what you want is by hard work and/or good luck, this is not something that sits well.

What if it's true though?

What if, by concentrating your mind on your hopes and dreams, you really could pull them nearer to you?

Wouldn't that be something worth getting excited about and merit pursuing, even if there were only a tiny chance that it could actually work?

For those of you that have seen 'The Secret' or 'What The Bleep Do We Know' you will have an idea of what I'm talking about. You will also know that there are elements of scientific fact, we are not just talking about some weird concept dreamt up by somebody that has swallowed too many magic mushrooms.

There is no doubt that many people working in science dismiss the idea as fanciful, but then again there were many scientists that thought the world was flat, that man couldn't physically run the mile in under 4 minutes and, that smoking wasn't harmful, so that is no reason to dismiss an idea out of hand.

In 500 years time man will look back on today the way we now look back on medieval times. The way we live, the way we communicate, the way we travel, the way we treat disease etc will all be unrecognizable from how we do now.

I honestly do not know if manifesting truly works I've an open mind on the subject. However, I do know that many highly intelligent and learned people swear by it and I'm not prepared to dismiss and disrespect their opinions along with millions of Buddhists, Hindis, Taoists etc, just because it's all a bit weird and out of my comfort zone.

Question: What would you like to manifest into your life?

39
Beat Procrastination

"Procrastination is opportunity's assassin"

- Victor Kiam

I was talking to a lady who'd contacted me through my website about coaching, when she brought up the problem of procrastination. I said that this was a problem that I encounter frequently but if her procrastination was that bad she probably wouldn't have called me in the first place. She didn't laugh either.

So why is it that we procrastinate and we all do it from time to time?

My personal opinion is that it comes from a human desire to keep the status quo and shy away from change. Procrastination often leaves things exactly as they are, right up until the very moment that continuing to procrastinate causes us such problems that we have no choice but to act. Not exercising until we become ill, not cutting down on eating fatty foods until we become overweight, not writing that report until the boss is in our face and so on. This is all part of the pain and pleasure NLP Meta program, the belief that our actions are either designed to move us away from pain or towards pleasure.

What I would like to suggest is a simple strategy for stopping procrastination. It's simply the fake it until you make it strategy. This can be used in many areas of your life and can be incredibly successful if implemented with a sense of fun.

So what if next time you can't make some small decision, you just guess, you pick one route, one conclusion, or one outcome and stick to it. Forget whether it's the correct decision in the long run, that's not important, just celebrate that you've made one. Decide to pretend that you never procrastinate and stick with it for 3 or 4 weeks. It'll feel weird but that's ok, because it's only a game after all and you can always go back to the 'old' you at the end of the experiment.

Decision-making is like anything else in life, the more we do it, the better we get at it.

So by faking decisions you are sending a signal to your unconscious mind that you are good at this decision making stuff. In time you actually do become proficient at getting things done and it becomes ingrained so go ahead and try it out. Why are you still reading? You are meant to be trying this out!

Question: What decision have you been putting off that you could fake?

40
Learn From Your Mistakes

"Mistakes are a part of being human. Appreciate your mistakes for what they are: precious life lessons that can only be learned the hard way. Unless it's a fatal mistake, which, at least, others can learn from."

- Al Franken

Do you ever find yourself going to bed and being unable to sleep because the events of the day are replaying themselves in your head in an endless loop? Is this usually worse during times when things are not going quite to plan or you are under higher levels of stress than is normally the case?

This is a common problem for many people and it can be very frustrating, not to mention tiring, when half the night is spent trying to switch off your thoughts with little or no relief.

There is a process that I use with clients that can help in times like this. I must say at this stage that if you suffer from long term insomnia then it may be wise to consult with a medical doctor This process is only designed to help with short term problems mainly brought on by work concerns etc.

Firstly, you need to have a journal or diary to hand. If you haven't got one I would encourage you to buy one because you need to be writing stuff down.

Think of the day and any events that didn't go quite as you would have wished. When you have thought of at least one thing, write it down. If there is more than one thing, great, you can learn even more than you anticipated. Write them all down but don't go berserk, I don't want you feeling suicidal before we move onto the next stage, so no more than 3 things.

Then think of lessons that you can learn from them. What could you have done differently? What could you change next time? Think really hard. If you can learn from your mistakes then they are worth committing. It's only when we refuse to learn from them and repeat them ad nauseum that they become like millstones around our neck.

Write down as many things as possible, but be sure to write them down in a positive manner. It's very important during this exercise to be kind to yourself it's not an excuse to beat yourself up. We ALL make mistakes it's a part of being human; it's how we react to them that separate the successful from the also-rans.

Now that you have the errors and the lessons written down, think of some things that you did well. I don't care how small they are; you will have done some things well, so write at least 2 down. It may simply have been getting to work on time or cooking a pleasant dinner or something much more impressive.

It doesn't really matter what it is, just write it down whilst mentally telling yourself well done!

The final stage is the easiest of the lot. Underline the page because that day is done. You can forget about it and consign it to history because that is what it is.

There is an addendum to this process that can be useful if you are worrying about things that you have to do the following day. Write them down too. The moment you commit to paper that which needs to be done, you send a message to your unconscious that it will get done, that you wont forget about it and that you can now enjoy a good nights sleep.

Question: Can you learn more from your mistakes?

41
Even Coaches Use Coaches

"You don't have to be ill to get better"

- Wayne Dyer

I wanted to wrap up this book by reiterating my passion for coaching.

I'm very happy with my life. I love my job, my family and where I live but that doesn't mean it couldn't be better. I can and will become a better coach, I can and will become fitter, I can and will become more peaceful, I can and will become a better husband etc.

My coach makes me accountable. I am somebody that can easily slip into procrastination and I guess even laziness. I have no difficulty whatsoever in saying yes to an extra round of golf or bike ride when maybe I should be doing some writing or seeing a client. I like my work/life balance and working with my coach who knows my goals and aspirations helps me to maintain that.

I've never spoken to anybody that claimed that they didn't benefit from using a personal coach. Seriously, never.

So why don't more people use coaches?

I guess there are many answers to that varying from being unable to afford to hire one to not even being aware that they exist. Another major reason is that many people believe that there is something just around the corner that will finally make them happy. The new house, the flashy car, the vacation, the promotion or even the retirement. Whatever it is, they believe that external stimuli will make them happy and content. Nothing could be further from the truth.

A good coach can help you to appreciate that genuine happiness always comes from within. They can also give you the tools, or more accurately, help you find them within yourself, to make sure that you decide on how you feel and not external forces that are outside your control.

Question: What could a coach do for you?

42
Inspiration

The glory of friendship is not the outstretched hand, nor the kindly smile nor the joy of companionship; it is the spiritual inspiration that comes to one when he discovers that someone else believes in him and is willing to trust him

- Ralph Waldo Emerson

Originally there were only going to be 41 chapters in this book. Actually, that's not completely true, there were going to be 50, but when I re-read the manuscript 10 of them were rubbish (only 10! I hear you cry) so I tore them up in an artistic rant.

I wanted to finish off by listing some of the people that have inspired me to write this book and improve my own life. Without these people I guess I would still be working 80 hours a week and feeling terrible or maybe even worse, dead.

Some are authors; some trainers, some therapists and some are all of those. There are also one or two sales, marketing and business gurus hidden in there and some fictitious people that I made up for absolutely no reason other than it kept me entertained and chuckling to myself for 5 minutes.

There is a comprehensive list of the books and audio programmes that have been my greatest sources of inspiration over the last 10 years. You can view this list at www.adaringadventure.com

If this book has in anyway inspired you then I would encourage you to read or listen to the people that inspired me to inspire you to hopefully inspire some others with inspiring inspiration.

Ok, so here are some of my personal heroes and heroines not already mentioned in my acknowledgements in the order that I can see them on my bookshelves as I scan round my office.

Dr Wayne Dyer, Dr Deepak Chopra, Dr John Eliot, Dr Foster went to Gloucester, Dr Stephen Covey (a bit of a theme building here I think), Dr Richard Bandler, Virginia Satir, Steve McDermott, John Grinder, Meat Grinder, Michael Heppell, Jamie Smart, Jamie Not Quite As Smart, Seth Godin, Curly Martin, Jim Loehr & Tony Schwartz, Richard Carlson, Jack Canfield, Malcolm Gladwell, Dale Carnegie, Napoleon Hill, Napoleon Flat, Tony Robbins, Tom Peters, Peter Toms, Jim Rohn, Jeffrey Gitomer, Harry Beckwith, Derren Brown (even though he doesn't like NLP, I'll forgive him), Milton H Erickson and finally His Royal Highness The Dalai Lama.

I am sure there will be others that I will feel terrible for missing out but I guess I'll just have to learn to live with it.

I thank you for reading this, I hope it has made you think more deeply about what is important to you and I wish you every success and happiness during (and I cannot quite believe I am quoting lyrics from a Prince song but here goes anyway) this thing called life.

Cheers

Tim